EVANSTON · PUBLIC
LIBRARY

Purchase of this library
material made possible
by a contribution
to the Fund for Excellence

Manatees

A Buddy Book by
Deborah Coldiron

ABDO
Publishing Company

UNDERWATER
WORLD

VISIT US AT
www.abdopublishing.com

Published by ABDO Publishing Company, 8000 West 78th Street, Edina, Minnesota 55439.

Printed in the United States.

Coordinating Series Editor: Sarah Tieck
Contributing Editor: Michael P. Goecke
Graphic Design: Deborah Coldiron
Cover Photograph: Photos.com
Interior Photographs/Illustrations: Brandon Cole Marine Photography (pages 9, 15, 17, 23, 25, 27, 30); Clipart.com (pages 11, 12); Corbis (page 29); GeoAtlas (page 13); Minden Pictures: Tony Heald/NPL (page 19), Mike Parry (page 18), Photos.com (pages 7, 19, 21, 28); ZSSD (page 19)

Library of Congress Cataloging-in-Publication Data

Coldiron, Deborah.
    Manatees / Deborah Coldiron.
        p. cm. -- (Underwater world)
    Includes index.
    ISBN 978-1-60453-134-3
    1. Manatees--Juvenile literature. I. Title.

QL737.S63C64 2008
    599.55--dc22

                                                                    2008005048

Table Of Contents

The World Of Manatees

Every living creature needs water. Some animals not only need water, they live in it, too.

Scientists have found more than 250,000 kinds of plants and animals living underwater. And, they believe there could be one million more! The manatee is one animal that makes its home in this underwater world.

Water covers 70 percent of Earth's surface.

Manatees are slow, gentle creatures. On average, adult manatees are about ten feet (3 m) long. They weigh about 2,000 pounds (900 kg).

FAST FACTS

Manatees are also known as sea cows.

Most manatees swim at speeds of three to five miles (5 to 8 km) per hour.

Manatees are found around the world. They can survive in fresh, salty, or **brackish** waters. They live in rivers, bays, and warm coastal waters.

These **mammals** take in air through their **nostrils**. Several times each hour, they go to the surface. There, they refill their large lungs.

Manatees close their nostrils when they dive. This prevents water from entering their lungs.

A Closer Look

Manatees are large and stout. They have rough, gray skin. And, they are often covered in **barnacles** or **algae**.

A manatee has two flippers near its front. Its tail is large, flat, and rounded. And short hairs cover its snout.

FAST FACTS

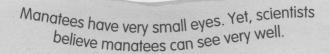

Manatees have very small eyes. Yet, scientists believe manatees can see very well.

The Body Of A Manatee

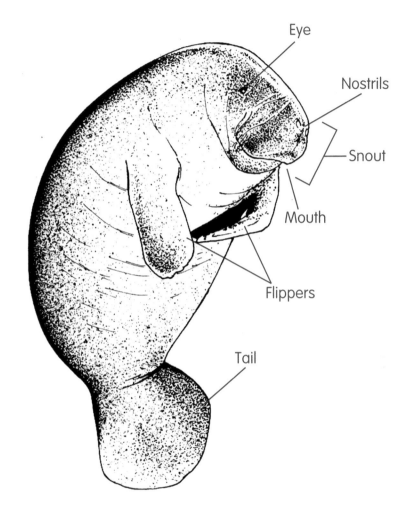

Eye

Nostrils

Snout

Mouth

Flippers

Tail

Three Species

West Indian manatee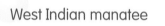

West African manatee

Amazonian manatee

There are three manatee **species**. They are very much alike. But, they live in very different places.

West Indian manatees are found near Florida's southeastern coast. They also live in the coastal waters of Central and South America.

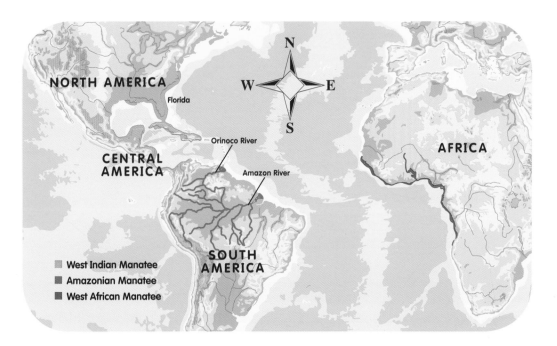

West Indian Manatee
Amazonian Manatee
West African Manatee

Amazonian manatees live in the Amazon and Orinoco rivers of South America. They are the smallest of the three **species**.

West African manatees are similar in size and **habitat** to West Indian manatees. But, they live off of Africa's western coast.

A Growing Manatee

Every two to five years, an adult female manatee may give birth. A mother carries a calf inside her body for about one year. When it is born, the calf is about three feet (1 m) long. It weighs about 65 pounds (29 kg)!

Manatee mothers and calves communicate using chirps, squeaks, and grunts.

Like other **mammals**, a manatee calf drinks milk from its mother after birth. A calf may drink its mother's milk for two years.

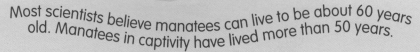

A manatee calf drinks milk from behind its mother's flippers.

Family Connections

Manatees have relatives in and out of the water. Underwater, manatees are only related to dugongs. On land, manatee relatives include elephants, aardvarks, and hyraxes.

There is only one dugong species in the world. These marine mammals look similar to manatees. But, they have smoother skin. And, males have two short tusks in their mouths.

Elephants are the biggest land mammals in the world. They have long trunks. Trunks help elephants drink, bathe, and pick up objects.

Aardvarks have long, thin snouts. These African mammals hunt by night and rest by day. They use their snouts to suck up termites and ants.

Hyraxes are also called coneys. These small land mammals are covered in fur. They live in Africa and Asia.

Dinnertime

Manatees eat only plants. But, sea grasses do not provide a manatee with much energy. So, they must eat large amounts to survive.

Each day, a manatee spends hours eating. Scientists say a manatee may eat more than 100 pounds (45 kg) of plants each day!

FAST FACTS

Breaking down tough sea grasses is a big job. So, an adult manatee's intestines are about 130 feet (40 m) long!

Manatees eat many types of plants, including water hyacinths.

Manatees have mouths full of molars. These teeth help them grind and chew their food.

Still, rough grasses and bits of sand are hard on their molars. Luckily, manatees constantly grow new teeth.

When a tooth in the front gets worn down, it falls out. Then, other teeth shift forward to close the gap in front. And, new teeth begin to grow in back.

The muscles in a manatee's lips are very strong.

A World Of Danger

Manatees do not have any natural predators. But, they are still not safe in their underwater home.

Manatees are **endangered**. So, laws protect them from hunters. Yet, their worldwide population remains low.

Florida's Chassahowitzka National Wildlife Refuge is a protected manatee habitat.

Many manatees are hurt or killed by boat **propellers**. Some die in the lock systems used to control floodwaters. Others are hurt after swallowing fishing hooks or trash.

Loss of **habitat** is one of the greatest problems facing manatees. Pollution and human traffic make some areas unsafe. And, chemicals harm manatee food sources.

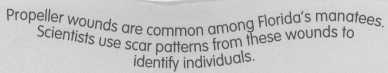

Propeller wounds are common among Florida's manatees. Scientists use scar patterns from these wounds to identify individuals.

Manatees are curious creatures.
This sometimes leads to boat
propeller injuries.

Fascinating Facts

❯ Manatees do not have eyelashes. Instead, a protective membrane covers each eye.

Usually, manatees travel alone. But they sometimes form groups.

❯ Manatees and dugongs are the only plant-eating **mammals** that spend their entire lives in water.

❱ At one time, some fishermen believed in mermaids. Today, many people think the tired sailors were actually seeing manatees!

❱ Manatees sleep just below the water's surface. Their **nostrils** remain above water so they can breathe.

Manatees can stay underwater for up to 20 minutes. But, most surface every few minutes for air.

Learn And Explore

In Florida, people are working to save manatees from **extinction**.

In 1981, singer Jimmy Buffet and Florida governor Bob Graham started the Save the Manatee Club. People adopt manatees through paid memberships. The money raised helps protect manatees and their **habitats**.

FLORIDA

MAR

95 FL
02302468

HAK 859

Save the Manatee

Many people in Florida joined the effort to protect manatees.

IMPORTANT WORDS

alga a plant or plantlike organism that lives mainly in the water.

barnacle a crustacean that spends its adult life permanently attached to something, such as rocks, boats, or other sea animals.

brackish somewhat salty.

endangered in danger of no longer existing.

extinction no longer existing.

habitat a place where a living thing is naturally found.

mammal any of a class of warm-blooded beings with a backbone that usually have hair and the females produce milk to feed their babies. Human beings, dogs, and whales are all mammals.

nostril either of the outer openings in the nose.

propeller a device that has a revolving central part with blades. The spinning blade moves a vehicle.

species living things that are very much alike.

WEB SITES

To learn more about manatees, visit ABDO Publishing Company on the World Wide Web. Web sites about manatees are featured on our Book Links page. These links are routinely monitored and updated to provide the most current information available.

www.abdopublishing.com

INDEX